Money Saving Tips

Cut Unnecessary Spending And Save Money With These Saving Tips

Table of Contents

Introduction 3

Chapter 1: Budgeting Is the First Step To Saving Money 4

Chapter 2: How To Save And Still Enjoy Good Food 7

Chapter 3: Save Money While Living A Comfortable Life 14

Chapter 4: Dress Well Without Splurging 26

Chapter 5: How To Save Money On Your Car Expenses 30

Chapter 6: Make Fun A Part Of Life Without Breaking The Bank.. 36

Chapter 7: Save Money While Taking Care Of Your Health.. 39

Chapter 8: Do Not Be Overburdened By Your Taxes 42

Conclusion 45

Introduction

This book contains proven steps and strategies on how to effectively save more money, so you no longer need to struggle to live paycheck to paycheck. Even during difficult times, you and your family do not need to suffer and live a deprived life. You can take control of your finances and provide for your family. The tips and techniques included in this book are easy to implement, so you can start saving money in all areas of your life. Always keep in mind that you deserve to be financially free. It is up to you to claim the independence.

Thanks again for purchasing this book. I hope you enjoy it!

Chapter 1: Budgeting Is the First Step To Saving Money

Planning and sticking to a personal budget can be tedious. Actually, a lot of people dread budgeting as much as they dread going to the dentist. Unfortunately, you do need to take time to design and adhere to a budget, but the benefits of doing so are infinitely greater than the costs.

Budgeting is the first step to saving money. A budget is your guideline in spending your hard-earned money to make sure you save money and only spend what you can afford. This technique ensures a surplus you can use to pay off any existing debts or save for the future.

When you live on a budget, you must make careful decisions about how you spend your money. You will not be tempted to make impulse purchases because each purchase or payment is made based on an objective decision-making process. Another advantage of having a personal budget plan is that you can allocate your limited funds to both your present needs and your future goals like retirement, your children's college education or even your own home. When you do not have a budget, it is quite easy for your funds to slip through your hands, and you end up barely making ends meet. Hence, saving money is an excellent endeavor.

However, you need to make a plan for the money you have saved. Do not be scared of budgeting because it is simply a tool there to help you. When creating your own personal budget, you will have a better understanding of your own personal financial status:

- Your total cash inflow every month from salaries, income from your own business, pension, and other passive income.

- Your total cash outflow every month for your household and other living expenses, payments of any outstanding debts, investments and other cash outlay. You may need to track your monthly expenses for a couple of months to determine the average amount of your total cash outflow. Make sure you also take into account all the bills that are not paid on a monthly basis such as insurance premiums and tuition fees. It is also ideal to include entertainment expenses in your list of cash outflows. Just because you have a budget does not mean you should forego all fun activities. Also include estimates for medical bills and other emergency situations. Estimate an annual amount, and then divide it by 12 to get your monthly budget.

- Your net cash flow every month. If this is positive, it means you spend less than you earn. You can then decide what to do with the surplus. You can start building your retirement fund, or you can start saving for your emergency fund or even a grand vacation for your family. Having a budget gives you total control over your finances. On the other hand, if your monthly net cash outflow is negative, you are spending more than you earn. You need to go back to your list of monthly expenses and other cash disbursements to see which areas you can cut back on. You can use the techniques and strategies discussed in this book to reduce your cash outflow, so you ultimately have a positive net cash flow every month.

Personal budgeting can be tedious and unexciting, but if you do it correctly, it can be very useful in reducing your financial stress and giving you peace of mind. No matter what your financial situation currently is, you will become more empowered to improve your situation once you have your finances under control.

Chapter 2: How To Save And Still Enjoy Good Food

You hear a lot of reasons why prices of food products continue to rise – increasing prices of oil, poor crop harvests, weak economy and even global warming. Yet, this does not mean you and your family should suffer and go without proper nutrition. Here are useful tips and techniques you can follow to save money on your food expenses without becoming malnourished.

Plan ahead.

Make it a habit to take inventory of the items available in your pantry and refrigerator, so you do not overbuy. Sit down with your family at least once a week to plan your weekly menu, and create a detailed grocery list from there. Planning your meals also enables you to plan on eating any leftover foods.

Before you head to the grocery store, make sure you are not hungry. Grab a quick snack if you need to. This helps you fight off any temptations to buy items not included in your grocery list, especially the expensive items displayed at the end of the aisles.

Prior to preparing your weekly menu plan, browse through ads to check food items that are on sale and coupons you can use to get discounts. There are also a lot of online sites you can join to receive regular alerts on available coupons from your favorite stores.

Choose healthy.

Contrary to what many people believe, eating healthy food can actually help you save money. This is based on the research study printed on the Journal of the American Dietetic Association. The research study showed that families who decided to go on a weight loss diet dropped weight and food expenses. They saved from the reduced portion sizes and from purchasing fewer high calorie foods. What many people do not realize is that they waste a lot of money on buying those "extra" foods that only add empty calories. These foods include chips, soda drinks and bakery goods.

You receive more for your money if you choose to buy foods with higher nutritional value for the price. For instance, instead of buying flavored drinks and sodas full of empty calories, you can opt to replace them with cheaper sparkling water you can splash with 100% natural fruit juices.

It is ideal to compare prices of food based on the quantity of servings you get with the nutritional value the food offers. For instance, with one pound of peaches, you can have three to four servings. When you divide the total price per pound by the number of servings, you realize the price is actually reasonable. Remember, you need to look for food that is heavy in nutrients and light in calories. The cheapest nutritious foods normally come fresh, canned or frozen.

This does not mean you must altogether forego eating sweet foods. You can still satisfy your sweet cravings by buying seasonal fruits instead of cookies and cakes, which are high in calories. Aside from being fat-free, fruits are also rich in nutrients and are a natural source of energy. You can also look for coupons or discounts for frozen yogurt (non-fat) or light ice cream, so your family can better enjoy the fruits as dessert.

Purchase produce that are in season.

The food section in most newspapers normally show which fresh produce is currently in season. These food products are commonly sold at lower prices because of higher supply. For instance, a corn on a cob sells at 10 cents per ear during the summer season. The same item is priced at around $1 during other months of the year. You can also shop at the farmers' market in your local area to get the best deals on local harvests. You do not even have to pay shipping costs.

Take advantage of coupons and sales.

Planning the meals to cook during the week based on food products that are on sale can definitely reduce your food expenses. You save even more if you use coupons on those sale items. You just need to ensure you stick to buying things you really need and plan to use immediately. If you have not tried couponing before, the best place to start is the Sunday newspaper, which is always filled with sale leaflets and coupons.

"BOGO" or buy one, get one free is the most common coupon you can get, and it enables you to purchase two products at the price of one. Just make sure you properly organize your stockpile, so you can implement the "FIFO" or first in, first out rule – use the products you bought earliest before using the products you purchased at a later date.

Bring your own lunch.

Preparing your own lunch and bringing it with you is one of the best ways to save money on food. It is also a brilliant method of using leftover food for your meals outside the house. Bringing your own lunch not only helps you save money, but it also enables you to control your food intake like the portion and calories of your meals. There are a lot of packed meals you can make from simple sandwiches to salads, soups, wraps or even hearty snacks of cheese. If you do not have access to a fridge in your workplace or at school, pack your lunch using freezer containers to help keep your food at the right temperature.

Discover the wonders of canned, dried and frozen foods.

During your next meal planning session, try including canned, dried and frozen foods in your recipes. These food items may be cheaper compared to fresh produce, but they are equally nutritious. Fresh produce is normally canned, dried or frozen when it is most ripe and packed with nutrients.

Poultry and fish products are normally flash-frozen to reduce storage/freezer damages and maintain their freshness. Working with frozen foods can also be economical because you can use only the quantity you need for cooking and save the rest. When you know how to properly store frozen foods, you will waste much less food.

Canned foods are normally bathed in salty water, syrup or juice. Because of that, you need to rinse them before eating or using them in cooking. Dried foods are dense in flavor, and they are good alternatives for fresh fruits. You may also opt to use evaporated or powdered milk when making soup, casseroles, mashed potato or dessert. Always try to buy foods in forms that allow you to get the best price for your specific requirements.

Use protein substitutes.

Poultry, fish, pork and beef are good sources of protein, but they are normally more expensive compared to the vegetarian sources of protein such as legumes, beans, tofu and eggs. You can try using alternative sources of protein in different days of the week. The vegetarian sources of protein are also good sources of fiber and other healthy nutrients from plants. Eggs are a cheap protein source you can eat any time of the day.

If you really want to include fish, meat or poultry in all your meals, use smaller portions and simply extend your dish with beans, vegetables, eggs and whole grains. When purchasing meat products, choose lean cuts such as "round" or "loin" for beef.

Avoid wasting food.

Before purchasing any perishable food items, make sure you have a specific purpose for it. According to the Environmental Protection Agency, Americans produce around thirty million tons of food waste on an annual basis. Instead of letting your food spoil, use leftover meat, vegetables and poultry when making casseroles, soups, salads and stews. You not only reduce your food expenses, but you can also explore your creativity in cooking. For instance, instead of simply reheating the leftover roasted chicken for dinner, you can mix it with salad vegetables. You can serve a loaf of dinner rolls, and your family can enjoy a nutritious and delicious meal that is easy on your budget.

Explore generic brands.

Choose to buy store brands rather than the national brands, which are normally more expensive. You get the same nutrition and quality because all food companies are required to adhere to strict standards in ensuring safe and high quality food and beverage products. What grocery companies normally do is purchase national brand products that were manufactured based on their specifications, and they simply place their own brand label on the products. Instead of looking at the brand name, check the list of ingredients on the packaging label to ensure you are getting the best, most nutritious deal. Take note that food companies are required to list down the ingredients according to weight. This means that when you purchase canned tomatoes, the list should have tomatoes first and not water.

Purchase prepackaged foods only when you need them.

Prepackaged foods including fresh fruits and vegetables that have been washed and sliced are always more expensive compared to raw products. Only buy these items when you are using a coupon for it or when the products are on sale. If you only need a small portion of a perishable item for your menu for the week, it is sometimes ideal to simply buy prepackaged foods at smaller quantities to produce less waste.

Purchase and cook your foods in bulk.

If there is a shopping club such as Costco or Sam's near your house, it can be economical in the long run to become a member. As long as you use your bulk purchases, they are an effective way to save on your food expenses. You may also check out your local area to see if there are shopping cooperatives that offer food items in bulk at a considerable discount. You not only save money when you cook your meals in time, but you save a lot of time, as well. You can cook your meals in bulk, and place them in the freezer in family-sized servings. Then, you can easily heat them at a later time.

Start your own garden.

Growing your own food is advantageous not only in saving money. You and your family can also enjoy fresh foods grown directly from your own backyard. If you do not have space for a garden, you can always plant tomatoes and other herbs in a container. If you have not done any gardening before, start with plants and herbs that are simple to grow. You can add more plants to your garden as you become more comfortable gardening.

Chapter 3: Save Money While Living A Comfortable Life

Here are useful techniques on how to easily reduce your household expenses without sacrificing your comfort and lifestyle. Some of the techniques below will enable you to make instant savings, but there are also others that will require some patience before you see any positive results. Still, some of the techniques necessitate an initial cash outlay, so you can enjoy considerable reduction in your household expenses in the long run.

Electricity

- Tell all members of your family to turn off the lights when leaving a room.

- Make it a habit to unplug your electronic gadgets and appliances when they are not in use. Even electronics that are turned off can consume electricity when they remain plugged.

- Regularly clean your light bulbs and light fixtures to remove any obstruction that may lessen their light output.

- During daytime, open your curtains to allow the natural light into your house.

- As much as possible, opt for a halogen or florescent light instead of a regular light bulb. Florescent lights are more expensive, but their long-term benefits far outweigh the initial costs. When compared to a regular light bulb, a florescent light has three times more energy

Money Saving Tips

efficiency, it is four times brighter, and can be used ten times longer.

- Try using wall paint or wallpapers that are light in color, so your rooms look brighter. It also enables your light bulbs to release up to 50 percent less light compared to when they are used in darker rooms.

Gas or Electric Cooling and Heating

- Ensure your air conditioning units are properly maintained, so they can sustain their efficiency. Your AC has to work harder and thus consumes more energy when there is a lot of dirt and other debris in the fan.

- Regularly inspect your insulation. When your house is properly insulated, you can reduce both your cooling and heating expenses because you can stop the air from escaping. Regularly check your insulation to make sure that it covers all of the 2x4s.

- Use a thermostat that is programmable, so you can automatically set your thermostat to your preferred temperature, even when you are sleeping or away from home. As a rule of thumb, the ideal temperature is 65 degrees Fahrenheit during the winter season and 80 degrees Fahrenheit during the summer season.

- Always check the doors and windows around the house for any air leakages. To make sure air inside the house does not escape, you can use a door sweep or caulking to fix any air leaks.

- Always keep your laundry room door shut during the summer months to stop the dryer from warming up your home. You can keep the laundry door open during the winter months to allow some heat to enter the rest of the house.

- Make sure your ventilating fans are turned off when not in use. Leaving the ventilating fans in your bathroom and kitchen on can waste a lot of energy because they take cooled or heated air from the room.

- Also make sure all your doors are kept shut to prevent your air conditioner or heater from working too hard.

- If you have a fireplace at home, consider not using it to save money. You can opt to have it plugged or sealed. If you want to cozy up using your fireplace, make sure the seal on the flue damper is tightened up.

- Consider investing in a ceiling fan because they help circulate air inside your room. This also prevents your air conditioner or heater from working too hard.

- Close the vents in rooms that are seldom used. Also, ensure your thermostat is not inside a room with closed vents because that can use up a lot of energy too.

Water

- Make a habit of turning off the water while you brush your teeth, shave or wash your hands. You waste around four gallons of water for each minute the faucet is left running.

- Always inspect all pipes and faucets inside and around your home to make sure there are no leaks. If you find any leaking faucet or pipe, make sure it is fixed immediately. You can check if your toilet has a leak by putting in a non-staining food color to the water tank. There is a leak when you see the food color flowing to the toilet bowl.

- Take your showers as quickly as possible to save water. You can also install an aerator or other water-saving devices on the showerhead.

- When you wash the dishes by hand, turn off the faucet while you rinse. You can save water by filling up both sections of the sink and using one section for washing and the other section for rinsing. When cleaning big dirty pans and pots, do not try to loosen the thick grime by running the pots and pans under the water. Instead, fill them up with soapy hot water and allow them to soak for an hour or two.

- Do you know you waste a lot of water when you turn on your faucet and wait for the water to warm up? You can install a rapid-delivery hot water device on your faucet, so the water heats up in less than fifteen seconds.

Gasoline and Miscellaneous Expenses

- Take advantage of the regular energy audits offered for free by power companies. You can call your local power company to request an inspection of your home to see how you can further cut your electricity bill. They even give you informational pamphlets on how to save energy.

Money Saving Tips

- Opt for a tankless water heater. Some people do not like tankless water heaters because they heat water instantly, and thus consume more energy when used. However, since it does not store water, you can save more because the water heater does not heat your water 24 hours a day.

- If you use a dual faucet (hot and cold), ensure you always turn on the faucet from the cold side. Starting with the hot side consumes a lot of energy since you will always be starting up the water heater.

- Reducing the temperature on your water heater even by a couple of degrees can mean a lot of savings on your electricity bill. In addition to that, you can also prolong the lifespan of your water heater by doing so.

- When you cook just for one, it is more energy-efficient to use a microwave, toaster oven or electric instead of your stove or oven.

- Do you know that a lot of electricity is normally used up during the preheating of an oven? If you plan to cook a dish for less than one hour, limit your preheating to only five minutes. If you plan to cook for more than one hour, preheating is often not required.

- When you want to heat your food, opt for a microwave oven rather than a conventional one because a microwave oven can save up to 50 percent of electricity.

- A lot of people are also not aware that most energy companies also have off-peak hours where energy consumption is billed at a lower rate.

Money Saving Tips

Contact your electricity company to know the off-peak hours in your local area, so you can schedule most of your tasks requiring electricity (such as washing, drying and pressing clothes) during those times.

Dryer

- Always clean the lint tray of your dryer. Make this a habit prior to using the drying because it helps in allowing the air to properly flow. The benefit is not only that your dryer will require less time to dry your clothes, but your dryer will have a longer lifespan, as well.

- It is a misconception that you save energy when you overload your dryer, so your clothes dry all at once. This does not give your dryer adequate space for the wet clothes to tumble well. You actually require more time drying your clothes when the dryer is overloaded.

- Dry delicates separately from clothes made of heftier materials. When you do this, you prevent your dryer from overheating, which saves energy in the end.

- During the summer months, take advantage of the hot weather by hang-drying your clothes. This saves energy from using the dryer less and lowering the temperature inside the house.

- Start using a gas dryer rather than an electric one, because gas dryers are more energy-efficient.

- Note that items made of heavier materials such as towels and jeans retain more water compared to regular clothes. You can reduce the drying time

Money Saving Tips

by putting these heavy clothes through an additional spin cycle before drying.

- A good technique to reduce your drying time by as much as 25 percent is throwing in a clean dry towel into the dryer before drying heavy clothes. The clean dry towel helps absorb the moisture from the hefty fabrics.

- Be careful in setting the temperature level in drying your clothes. Read the garment labels before throwing them into the dryer. Using excessive heat not only consumes more energy, but it can also damage your clothes.

Washing Machine

- Start using cold water when rinsing your clothes in the washing machine because it has the same effect as warm or hot water.

- If you notice your clothes are still not thoroughly clean after you washed them either in cold or hot water, pre-soak them in warm water to loosen the dirt. This is particularly useful for children's clothes, which can become heavily soiled. Pre-soaking can also reduce your need to wash the clothes using hot water.

- Just like with the dishwasher, it is ideal to use the washing machine only when the load is full. If you need to wash your clothes but cannot make a full load yet, ensure your washing machine is set to the right load size to conserve electricity and water.

- Do not use a lot of detergent, so you can save on both energy and water in rinsing your clothes.

Money Saving Tips

- Place your washing machine near the water heater since the nearer the washing machine is to the water heater, the less heat escapes through the pipes.

- Insulate any exposed piping from the washing machine to the water heater. This reduces the heat lost from the pipeline.

Dishwasher

- As much as possible, do not use the dry cycle on your dishwashing machine. Instead, hand dry your dishes or allow them to drip dry. You can stop the dry cycle by doing a reset of the dishwasher setting or manually stopping the dry cycle after the rinse cycle is completed.

- Before using the dishwasher, try to accumulate as many soiled dishes as you can, so you can fill the dishwasher to its capacity. Using the dishwasher with smaller loads uses a lot of energy from heating the water.

- The rinse hold feature of most dishwashers normally utilizes an additional three to seven gallons of hot water for every wash. Do not use the rinse hold, as often as possible.

- Instead of using the pre-rinse feature of your dishwasher, you can pre-soak dishes with heavy dirt in warm water with detergent. This is enough to loosen the stains and grime prior to putting the dishes into the dishwasher.

- The longer the wash cycle is, the more energy your dishwasher consumes. You should, therefore, use the appropriate wash cycle for the size and level of dirtiness. If you are washing lightly soiled dishes, simply choose the shortest wash cycle.

Refrigerator

- When you want to thaw frozen foods, keep them inside the fridge to regulate the temperature inside and help the fridge to work less.

- Position your fridge far from any sources of heat like the oven, the dishwasher or even direct sunlight. When your refrigerator is placed near a source of heat, its compressor works harder. This consumes more energy.

- Also, ensure there is adequate clearance around your fridge for better heat dispersal and air circulation. For proper operation, give your refrigerator a minimum two-inch clearance on every side.

- Allow your cooked food to cool down prior to placing it inside the fridge. Your refrigerator must work harder when hot food is placed inside because it compensates for the additional heat.

- Always check the temperature inside the refrigerator to ensure it is not set at a very low temperature. The ideal temperature inside the fridge is around 36 to 40 degrees Fahrenheit while the ideal temperature inside the freezer is around zero to five degrees Fahrenheit.

- Stop the habit of deciding what to get inside the fridge while the door is open. Decide on what to get before you even open the fridge or freezer door to prevent the cold air from escaping. As much as possible, try to shorten the amount of time the fridge door is open.

- Ensure that both the freezer and refrigerator are not packed beyond capacity. An over-packed freezer has less efficiency while an over-packed refrigerator has poor air circulation.

Communication

- Try using the internet to communicate as much as possible. Rather than sending text messages or calling, you can simply send an instant message or email over the internet.

- Consider consolidating your communication tools into one service provider, so you can get a bulk discount for your cell phone, internet and landline phone services. This also saves you time when paying the bills because you only have to track one bill.

- At least once every year, compare prices from different service providers for your internet, landline phone and cell phone needs. The communication market is quite competitive and these companies often try to outdo each other by offering better rates.

- Regularly assess your billing statements to see if there are any service features you can do away with. For instance, if you rarely use call waiting or call forwarding, cancel those features to lower your monthly expenses. You can also assess the number of text messages you send out and the number of calling minutes you make every month. If you are using less than what is available in your mobile plan, change it to a lower and cheaper plan.

- Assess whether you still need both your land line and cell phone. If you use your land line for less than five times every month, cancel it. This way you do not pay for a service you do not use.

Credit Cards

- Consolidate all your existing debts. If you are using several credit cards, transfer the outstanding balances to the credit card with the lowest interest rate. You can also avoid paying late penalty charges when you consolidate your debts because you will have fewer due dates to track.

- Reduce your interest expenses. You can do this by calling up your credit card company to request an interest reduction for your high interest credit cards. This is normally possible for credit card holders in good standing.

- Take advantage of zero percent interest. This is one of the best ways to reduce your interest expenses on your credit cards. A lot of credit card companies offer zero percent introductory interest rate when you transfer the outstanding balances from your other credit cards.

- Avoid paying late fees and other penalty charges. The best technique to do this is to pay the minimum amount immediately after you receive your credit card bill. If have extra funds at the end of the month, you can make additional payments to your credit card to reduce the interest charged to your outstanding balance.

- You can try using a prepaid debit card for your regular expenses rather than a credit card. Based

Money Saving Tips

on your budget, you can load your debit card directly from your savings account with the amount you use for buying groceries, gasoline and other expenses you can pay with a card. Prepaid debit cards can stop you from overspending since you are restricted to the balance of your card.

Chapter 4: Dress Well Without Splurging

Have you ever experienced looking into your closet filled with clothes and still feel like you have nothing to wear? It is quite hard to create a wardrobe you love while sticking to a budget within your means. It is especially hard when you are forced to settle for clothes you do not like because the price is right for you. When you are working with a tight budget, shopping for the right clothes can be a challenge.

This challenge becomes even bigger for parents who are responsible for their own clothes and for the entire family's clothes, but do not fret. There are things you can do to shop on a budget and still create a wardrobe you and your family want to wear.

- Start shopping ahead for the upcoming seasons. Retail stores are known for their quick turnover of clothing lines. If you are prepared to plan for the upcoming seasons, you can take advantage of the great deals offered by many stores. This is mostly applicable to adults since we normally buy the same sizes, but you can also try doing this for your children by approximating the sizes they will wear. If you are not sure what size to buy for your children and want to shop for them for the following year, buy clothing a size or two bigger than what they currently wear.

  Here is a simple guideline on which clothes to buy on specific months:

  - January: Stock up on winter clothing, including coats and sweaters. You can also choose to buy your apparel for the next holiday.

- April: Stock up on Easter and spring clothes.
- May: Buy athletic clothing.
- July: Purchase swimwear and other summer apparel.
- October: Buy back-to-school clothes for your kids and fall apparel for the whole family.

• Give your old clothes new life. You can hold "clothes swapping parties" with your close friends. Everyone can bring a few clothes they are willing to part with. Then, each of you can exchange your clothes for the clothes of your friends. This way, all of you have "new" clothes at the end of the party.

• List the retail stores you always frequent to buy clothes. Then, visit the official websites of those stores and sign up to receive notifications and emails from them. Many retail companies have started using this as their major marketing tool. They normally send out money-saving coupons and incentives to their members on a regular basis. You can use those coupons on your next purchase.

• Join loyalty programs, which are basically rewards programs offered by retail companies to their loyal customers. By joining a loyalty program, you become eligible to receive various rewards like invitations to private promotions and coupons exclusive to members.

Money Saving Tips

- Start using coupons. Make your own coupon binder that you can fill with all the coupons you get directly from the stores or by mail. When you receive coupons through your email, immediately print those you think you will use and keep them in your coupon binder. When you are ready to go out shopping, simply flip through your coupon binder to see which coupons you can use. Also, ensure your coupons are organized by date, so you use the ones that expire the soonest. Always keep in mind that the secret to successful couponing is organization.

- Wait for the right timing to make your purchases. If you truly like a particular piece of clothing now, you will still like it at a later time. Stop yourself from making impulse purchases, and wait for the items to go on sale. There is a high likelihood that you will not be waiting for a long time. Retail companies always want to move their merchandise as quickly as possible. This means they mark down even brand new products pretty quickly. As much as possible, do not buy cloths at full price because you can always get them at a better price. Just set your expectations and know the size or color you want may no longer be available when the apparel goes on sale. You can always look for alternatives.

- Do your shopping with discount retails such as Marshalls, TJ Maxx and Ross. They sell apparel and other products at prices that are lower than what you normally find in other shops. These discount retailers can do so partly because they sell products that are one season or one year behind. They get their merchandise from other stores who could not sell them at full price.

Money Saving Tips

- Save money when buying clothes online by searching for savings codes at popular online sites such as CurrentCodes.com, CouponCabin.com and RetailMeNot. On these websites, you can browse through collections of online coupon codes, which can enable you to enjoy various perks like free shipping and discounts.

- Still, the best way to save money on clothes is to downsize and organize your wardrobe. Every time you do so, you will be amazed by the amount of clothes and accessories you actually have. You will realize there are certain pieces of clothing you have forgotten about that you can use again to spice up your wardrobe.

Chapter 5: How To Save Money On Your Car Expenses

It is possible to save a huge amount of money on your automotive expenses. Your savings can be as high as a couple thousand dollars per year. The more cost-saving efforts you implement, the more money you can have at the end of the year. The actual amount of savings people have normally varies extensively depending on their personal situations.

New Vehicle Purchases

- Try keeping your vehicles for longer periods of time rather than trading them in every few years. You not only spend more money when you regularly trade cars in because the prices of new vehicles increase every year but also because vehicles depreciate rapidly. When you trade your vehicles in, you lose money on the low trade-in values you get. Instead, purchase vehicles that have good quality, so you can keep them for five to seven years.

- When you are planning to buy a new vehicle, purchase a smaller model because they are usually cheaper compared to the bigger ones. Since a small vehicle is lighter, it also consumes less gas. Add to that the cheaper insurance for a small vehicle, and you save even more.

- Before you agree to any additional options for your new car, consider the effects those add-ons have on your gasoline usage. For instance, when you use air conditioning, you use up more

Money Saving Tips

gasoline. An automatic transmission also lessens your miles per gallon when compared to manual transmissions. The same is true when you get a 6-cylinder engine. You can have a higher gas mileage with a 4-cylinder engine.

- When buying a new vehicle, do not purchase credit disability or credit life insurance from your car dealer. You need to be firm even if your car dealer is insistent because they normally give higher prices for this insurance coverage. It is advisable to obtain standard life and disability insurance through your employer, or if you are self-employed, get an individual insurance policy.

- Have extreme caution when buying an extended warranty or service contract on your new vehicle through the car dealer. Many sales dealers oversell these contracts, which actually have pretty limited coverage only. You save a lot more money when you buy these service and extended warranty contracts directly from the service providers such as Warranty Direct.

Car Maintenance

- It is always advisable to keep your vehicle well-tuned. Using a poorly tuned vehicle costs you around 25 to 33 percent more gasoline expenses. It is definitely more inexpensive to pay for regular tune-up.

- For every 3,000 miles, change both the oil and oil filter in your vehicle, even though the owner's manual of your car suggests a lower frequency. Many experts advise frequent oil changing because it is considered the single most vital element in extending the life of your car engine.

Money Saving Tips

The benefits you get from frequent oil changes are greater than the cost of constant repair and engine deterioration.

- It is also a good idea to check the air filter of your vehicle every month. When you keep a dirty air filter, the life of your engine is shortened and your gasoline mileage can be reduced by as much as 10 percent. It is really simple to clean your air filter. You can do it by removing it and then blowing it using an air hose. If you need to, replace your air filter, so it can function better.

- Start using radial tires that are steel-belted to enhance your gas mileage by about 10 percent each year.

- You do not need to use octane gas higher than what your car's manual suggests. Premium gas does not really offer any advantage to most vehicles. You are better off with cheaper gasoline if you do not have a high-performance car engine and your car manufacturer does not suggest you use high-octane gasoline. Remember, premium gasoline can cost 10 to 15 percent more than regular gas.

- Make it a habit to regularly inspect your tire pressure. For each pound of under-inflation, you are actually consuming more gasoline – as high as six percent per mile.

- You can extend the mileage of your tires by a couple thousand miles when you have them balanced at least once per year. Tires that are improperly balanced run through treads more quickly, easily deteriorate your shock absorbers, and impair your suspension system. You do not want these things to happen because it means more expenses for you.

- It is also advisable to regularly inspect the fluid levels of your vehicle. When you run with a low water level, it can greatly shorten the life of your battery. In addition to water, regularly inspect your brake fluid, coolant, automatic transmission fluid and clutch fluid.

Gasoline

- Pump your own gas since self-serve gasoline is normally cheaper by 5 to 10 percent compared to full-service gasoline.

- When you pump gas, do not "top off the tank" because some of the gasoline might end up spilling over when you park on a hill or when the gas expands in the sun.

Car Insurance

- Inquire from your insurance agent how much savings you can have when you raise your deductible on your car collision insurance. Normally, when you increase the deductible from $250 to $500, you can have savings of around 10 to 30 percent. If you have maintained a good driving record, you can have even more savings.

- Ensure that your insurance company is promptly notified of all the safety features that can make you qualified for additional discounts on either your car or homeowner's insurance. Some of these safety features include smoke detector in your house and air bags or automatic seat belts in your vehicle. Even you are a non-smoker or non-drinker, you can enjoy extra discounts.

- If you are driving an older vehicle, you can opt to drop your comprehensive and collision coverage, but make sure you still have liability coverage. Collision coverage is normally a requisite when you have an unpaid auto loan, but if your older vehicle is already fully paid, you can compare the book value of your car against the collision premiums you have to pay. A vehicle that is more than 5 years old normally has a book value of less than $1,000. The amount you pay for your comprehensive and collision coverage may be a lot more than what you actually get.

- Prior to purchasing a new vehicle, confirm with your insurance agent if you will incur additional insurance expenses from buying a specific car model because of higher repair, damage and theft costs.

- Take your time to shop around for the best insurance. If you are already getting quality service from your existing insurance company and they offer good rates, you can always opt to stick with them, particularly when you have had previous car accidents or tickets. If you have a good driving record, it is advisable to shop around to see if there are other insurance companies who can give you a better rate.

- You can opt for combined policy for both your car and homeowner's insurance. Insurance companies normally give out good discounts for multiple insurance policies.

- Check if you qualify for the good student discount for your car insurance. You normally qualify if your household has a high school student or college student under 25 years old. You can save

Money Saving Tips

25 percent on your insurance when you qualify for the discount.

- Maintain a good driving record by avoiding tickets for moving violations. You can save as much as 20 percent if you have a good driving record for 3 years or more.

Driving

- Consider carpooling to work. You can save as much as $200 per year in gasoline alone when you share the driving with just other person. This is computed based on a 20-mile round-trip distance every day. When you carpool with two or more other people, you can increase your savings by even more. Aside from saving on gasoline expense, you also save on maintenance expenses and deterioration of your vehicle.

- Another advantage of carpooling is that you can reduce the yearly mileage on your vehicle. Because a lower mileage can reduce your risks of accident, you can pay a lower amount for the same insurance coverage for your vehicle.

- Do not let your car idle while warming it up. Your car engine warms up faster when you drive compared to when the engine is idle. Idling your car can waste around one quart of gasoline every 15 minutes.

- You can save on gasoline when you combine your errands into a single trip. As much as possible, do not backtrack when you run errands.

Chapter 6: Make Fun A Part Of Life Without Breaking The Bank

Working on a budget and saving money does not necessarily mean you will miss out on life. The reason you work is to enjoy life and what it can offer you and your family. Here are useful techniques you can follow to save money without completely eliminating "fun" from your life:

- If you enjoy watching movies, go out for a daytime matinee rather than watching a movie at the cinema at night. Make sure you have eaten a heavy lunch at home before heading to the movie theater, so you will be able to resist the temptations of splurging on soda or popcorn.

- You can definitely save more money when you do movie streaming over the Internet and watch in the comfort of your own home. You can also opt for a DVD rental service such as Redbox or Netflix.

- If you like eating out, you can avoid eating at full-price restaurants by hunting for discounts through social coupon services such as SaveMore, Groupon, LivingSocial and Scoutmob. Do not immediately throw away the restaurant-coupon flyers you get in the mail to see if there is anything that appeals to you.

- If you want to eat at specific restaurants that do not offer coupons or discounts, you can still save money by dining during their "happy hours." A lot of restaurants give out great dining deals on certain menu items during off-peak hours. Do not

Money Saving Tips

hesitate to call your favorite restaurant to inquire about their Happy Hour or specific day/night specials.

- If you are one of those people who consider shopping as entertainment, you can still avoid making this habit an expensive one. One effective way is to not bring your wallet when you have the urge to shop just for the sake of shopping. You can entertain yourself by window-shopping, admiring shoes and handbags, and gazing at fine jewelry without breaking the bank. You also need to be careful because excessive window-shopping may increase your desire to buy things that are not really within your budget. Window-shopping is a good alternative to spending money, but a lot better than window-shopping is looking for a different form of entertainment.

- If you like going to concerts, you do not need to spend a lot of money just to listen to the most popular bands. You can explore up-and coming artists who normally play free or low-priced gigs with the intention of gaining exposure.

- You can also check jazz clubs, coffee shops, nightclubs, street festivals, bars and city parks to see if they will be holding live performances. Major cities also normally give out discount tickets for symphonies. You can also get cheaper deals by buying tickets to watch symphony rehearsals instead of actual evening performances.

- If you like going to live comedy shows, you can definitely save money when you go to an amateur night where unknown talents take the stage with the hope that a talent scout will notice them. The

Money Saving Tips

tickets to these amateur nights are a lot cheaper compared to more experienced comedians. You can even get the tickets for free, but you need to check if you will be required to buy a minimum amount of food or drink to enjoy the amateur comedy shows.

- If you like watching sports events, you can save money by getting seats in the highest balconies that are normally sold at low prices. You might also be able to get inexpensive last-minute deals for a surplus seat as long as the game is not sold-out.

Chapter 7: Save Money While Taking Care Of Your Health

Even when you have medical insurance, health care expenses can become costly, but there are things you can do to save money on healthcare without putting you and your family's health in danger. The following useful tips can help in trimming your medical care expenses by hundreds of dollars, or maybe even more.

- Always ask questions. When you are prescribed to undergo several laboratory exams, it will not do you any harm to ask your doctor if all the tests are truly necessary. This is not an easy task, but if you are working with a tight budget, you need to voice your concerns. The first question that you can ask your doctor is "Why?" Have your doctor explain why the tests are required. Ask if the tests can be safely deferred while you wait for the symptoms to improve. A lot of medical diagnoses can be established by a doctor simply by listening to the patient and taking a good medical history. A thorough physical examination is also a good way to make proper diagnosis. Many doctors prescribe further testing when the symptoms are not clear to them, and they are looking at several possibilities.

- Take the time to shop around and compare prices. You can visit the website of Healthcare Blue Book, which provides free consumer guides to help you determine fair prices in your specific location for health care products and services. What you essentially need to do is to understand the costs of your healthcare prior to getting it. A lot of people who get insurance think that if they remain in-network, they will obtain the network discount and it will not matter where they obtain their healthcare. Understand that it truly matters. "In-network" pertains to a listing of health care providers who have entered into an agreement with the insurance company on the rates that will be charged for their specific services. In general, you will pay less for healthcare providers that are included in the listing, but it is still advisable to compare rates within the healthcare providers in the network. For instance, an insurance company normally pays an allowable amount ranging from $500 to $3,000 for the same MRI tests. Therefore, you must be cautious, so you do not pay more than you should.

- Make the most of online tools. There are a lot of online sites that provide comprehensive information (including symptoms and indications) on many diseases and medical conditions. It sometimes pays to visit these websites before rushing to an urgent care center or other medical clinics. The information can help you determine when it is safe to do self-treatment and when you have to consult a physician.

- As much as possible, try switching to generic drugs. The U.S. Food and Drug Administration stated that generic drugs have the same active components and that they have the same effects on the human body as brand-name medications at costs that can be lower by as much as 30 to 80 percent. Also, verify if you are qualified for any of the drug assistance programs offered by your local area or state. You can also contact pharmaceutical companies that manufacture your

Money Saving Tips

regular medications to see if they have any financial assistance programs you can use.

- Consult your physician about pill splitting, but do not attempt to split your pills without consulting your doctor for there are some risks to this practice. There are certain tablets that are not safe to split, especially time-released medications and capsules.

Chapter 8: Do Not Be Overburdened By Your Taxes

You need to learn how to take ownership of your income tax computation, so you can make sure you are not paying more than you should. There are a lot of deductible costs and expenses you can use to reduce your taxes. You will definitely save money on taxes if you know the deductions applicable to you. Aside from tax deductions, here are other techniques on how to lower your tax payable:

- See if you are qualified for the earned income tax credit, which is normally applicable to taxpayers belonging to the low to moderate income range. Earned income tax credits can give you tax credit of as much as $6,000. If your income is less than $50,000 per year, check if the tax credit applies to you. People most commonly qualify when they become new parents during the taxable year.

- Start your own business. You can improve your tax status when you become an entrepreneur because you will have greater control over the amount of taxes you pay. You have the option of retaining your income in the business to be used in operations rather than withdrawing it as your personal income. You can also use additional costs and expenses as deductions to your taxable income. If you plan to take this route, it is advisable to seek the assistance of a tax professional that is familiar with the latest laws on taxation, so you can properly plan your taxes.

- Benefit from your own kids. The tax laws offer several tax benefits that are applicable to parents.

Money Saving Tips

Some of these benefits include tax credit for child care expenses – the child tax credit can be as high as $1,000 for every child below 17 years old. The payments you make for alimony can also be used as tax deductions.

- Start placing funds into college savings. Not many parents take advantage of the tax benefits from the creation of 529 college savings accounts for their kids. On the condition that the money placed in that savings account will be used for college tuition, you will not be taxed on the earnings of your savings account.

- Consider keeping your mortgages for as long as you can since interest payments for mortgages can be used as tax deductions. However, you need to make sure that the tax benefit you get from the extended mortgage is not lower than the extra interest payments you incur. Of course, you also need to take into account the peace of mind you will have when you are debt-free.

- Start savings funds for your retirement. You may think it is troublesome for you to voluntarily lower your take home pay every month, so you can increase your retirement contributions. Yet, you will have more funds to spend when you finally retire.

- Donate more money. Aside from donations to charitable institutions, you can also claim gifts (up to $13,000) to individuals as tax deductions. You and your spouse can even give each of your kids up to $26,000 (referred to as "gift splitting") and use this as tax deductions.

Money Saving Tips

- Start tracking your medical expenses. There are particular expenses related to health care that can be used as tax deductions. These include acupuncture sessions, medical supplies such as bandage, and even breast pumps. You can visit irs.gov to see the complete listing of medical expenses you can deduct from your tax payable. Just ensure you keep all the receipts, which you may be required to present as supporting documents for your tax deduction claims.

- Start increasing your energy efficiency. The U.S. government urges its taxpayers to become more energy efficient by giving tax credits for a number of energy efficiency efforts such as purchase and installation of energy saving devices such as insulation, new doors and windows, and suitable cooling and heating systems. You can also claim as tax credits the purchase and installation of alternative sources of energy such as solar panels. You will not only save on your electricity bill, but you will also pay fewer taxes.

Conclusion

I hope this book was able to help you to learn how to take control of your finances while living the life you want for yourself and your family.

The next step is to start creating your own personal budget, if you still do not have one.

Thank you and good luck!

www.ingramcontent.com/pod-product-compliance
Lightning Source LLC
Chambersburg PA
CBHW070717180526
45167CB00004B/1511